I'm Lying, I Swear and other attempts at poetry

Tanvi

BookLeaf Publishing

Presentation by *BookLeaf Publishing*

Web: www.bookleafpub.com

E-mail: info@bookleafpub.com

ISBN: 9789357218313

First edition 2023

DEDICATION

To

my parents Ruchira and Manish Jain and my friends for giving me strength.

my teachers for always believing in me.

to Paromita ma'am, as promised. Thank you for the ice cream and waffles.

To the world around me for inspiring me,

And to you, the reader, for giving this book a chance.

ACKNOWLEDGEMENT

There are many people without whom this book would not have been possible, so I will thank them one by one.

Many thanks to Bookleaf Publishing for making it possible for this set of poems to migrate from a Google Doc to an actual book. Watching my own work go out there is both terrifying and exhilarating. Thank you for giving me this opportunity.

To my parents, thank you for not batting an eyelid when I told you I was publishing a book. Thank you for listening to my concerns and stresses on days when I felt this wasn't going to work out. Thank you always for your unconditional support and love and for being there for me no matter what.

To my talented friend Alagar, for helping me refine a lot of the ideas here. Your advice is always insightful.

To all my friends who have supported me, whether it is by proofreading the poems or providing me support and validation when I needed it (you know who you are), thank you so much.

Many many thanks to Teepa Snow, Polly Logan and Joanna Fix from Positive Approach to Care for allowing me the chance to view life from the perspective of people with dementia. Special thanks to Joanna for sharing so much about your life with me and helping me write a poem which would provide an accurate account of what a person with dementia experiences in their daily life.

PREFACE

This book has seen everything. The nights I cried over my laptop while typing through blurry vision. The days I felt all right for once, when the words flowed out of my good side. It has seen my bouts of arrogance, my fits of insecurity. It has seen the times I studied for ten hours and forced myself to write for two. It has seen the days I gave in and did nothing at all but write. It has seen the days I was too burnt out to get out of bed. It has seen and heard the fights and uncomfortable conversations I have had as a result of writing some of the poems in it.

It has seen all of me, even the ugliest parts, and showed me myself in return.

Writing this book in effectively a month has forced me to peel off the layers I built around myself. Once I ran out of fluff, I had to dig deep and mine my own truths for material. The good thing about that is it makes you cry, which is good. The bad thing about that is that it is now out there for the world to see and know. Strangely, of that I am now unafraid. Pain and struggle makes for decent poetry.

I've grown while writing this. I've fallen more in love with the act of writing, and I have realised I cannot live without it. It has given me purpose, forced me to re-evaluate my future.

The poems in this book experiment with structure and meaning. Some poems are meant to be read in a certain way, like most of the formally structured poems here, and some, such as Coffee in Ten, can be read any way you want. I have used some images and little artistic elements to add to the texture of the poems.

There is somewhat of an overarching theme in this book — a fluctuation of emotion : the huge, confusing feelings you feel as you grow up, the ones you don't know where to put or what to do with. Some poems are reserved, with mostly veiled meaning, and some are more robust. They all deal with a variety of topics, including dementia, academic pressure and trauma. I will place trigger warnings in the table of contents so that you may skip over those poems to avoid upset.

My privilege in being able to write and put this out there is not lost on me. There are far greater struggles, and some of these are mine. I entreat you to be kind.

Poetry —

Is it
Sunrays
blades through daybreak fog;
Perfumed air, transient
Imprinting on the senses.

Perhaps
diamonds on pitch black mink
burning through space
to settle, Glistening
at your throat.

Or
hot gold tumbling
leaf by leaf,
gloss on lips
of Moving trees.

drops of blood
Rubies; in my mouth
the bandage you clothe
my finger in ?

The universe it
s tr e e e...t c h e s.. . . . .
. .
fated, crashing
into itself
a Supernova

your eyes its centre.

Black ink I draw
from my
heart, my fingers
fountain pen, broken nib
strangled words, confused
offered to you
.
.
.
wilting hibiscus at your altar.

A Real Estate Agent's Lamentation

number 65 has sick green walls
moss and mould peeling **plasterwork**
the **front** : sad red door (brass knocker and two steps)
on your **left-hand** side you will see
forgotten drawing **under** the sofa
spider webs **or** tangled hair
please refrain from **noticing**
the mouse-nest in the fireplace.
quality real estate **there**, you see
it shifts and breathes, as for the shroud
whether it will lift again
i do not know
whether it will live again
i do not know[1]

---

[1] Footnote : Two friends and I decided to try out (a version of) the found//fount sonnet, pioneered by Desmond Kon Zhicheng-Mingdé, with a few optional modifications. The source text is a random passage picked from Paula Hawkins' *The Girl on the Train*. Each of us decided to write a found//fount sonnet based on the following conditions : a) all fourteen words had to be from that same paragraph b) the chosen words could appear anywhere in the poem, but each line had to contain one. The fourteen words I picked were : left-hand, under, number, it, there, noticing, I, the, whether, whether, front, I, or, plasterwork. Some words were repeated, but I still counted them in the 14 words for the sonnet.

I'm Lying, I Swear

When I was eight I ran over a butterfly
I swear I heard it scream.
Its mud-brown wings rent in three by the ruthless
rubber of my bike. A grease spot.

I swear
it wasn't on purpose
Butterflies are just so
fucking annoying.

Why do they have to be so breakable!!!!!!!!!!!! One
time
a boy in our colony held a butterfly by its wings
like a suspect being arrested. arms tearing at the
seams
And when the butterfly stopped writhing, released on
the ground
It went back to settle
on his chest.

So idiotic!

Last Sunday one sat on the snout of the dragon
on my hand-me-down wool sweater. I wanted to
scream. Butterflies are so stupid, they never learn
I could crush you so easily, accidentally even.
And yet to come to feed from my hand? Uninvited?

Fools—

Nature's folly in a hundred colours. A mockery of
everything
around them. So naïve. So god damn
Trusting.
They never learn, do they? Flying about like they
own the place (my home/the garden/the park/the
path/underneath my bicycle)
One time I saw a butterfly with a chewed-up wing.
Out of all the evolutionary beings I think they serve
the least purpose.
Like a broken lighthouse they only look pretty from
afar. pathetic

I only ever thought they were pretty when I saw
yellow ones playing in the mango trees
from a hospital window
I never saw them again. maybe they died
like they always do.

Sometimes I think butterflies
exist to be broken
(And sometimes I wish
I was one.)

The Time Capsule I Reinterred

in the garden of my childhood home i found
a rusted iron time capsule.photographs a watch some
sand a
letter.

faded photographs (six)

1. back of a woman on a beach
2. close up of woman's smile
3. two hands, almost touching
4. gold necklace splayed on skin
5. pile of clothes, foot in frame
6. an embrace.

watch frozen
in time (thirty past six) —
the sun beats harsh
on my skull.

yellowed paper
lip-print-sealed

anjali,
dearest
time will preserve
what we could
not.
yours,

prakriti

bright sunday summer afternoon
grass of my childhood home
soft dirt in my hair
daylight ripe
orange on my lids

i think of
water, dripping
down stairs,
feet and tangled hands
sand in cracks of floorboards.

“Before us? oh, you mean
before your grandfather moved in?
your grandmother lived here with her
best friend.”

Dear Childhood Friend

Not usually, on days when the rain is thick and lush
like the time we were eight and danced on the terrace
of our childhood apartment building :
I remember our Famous Five escapade.

I, the ringleader, looking for footprints on a key—!
You, older, humouring me.
That day we never found prints
Or who stole the mango-net.
Invisible
thread bound us as one.

Words fall so easily from me, natural
as soft winter sunlight — afternoon on the veranda
crossword puzzles and drying wet hair.
"I love you. Thank you for being my friend."
A message, sent across a thousand miles
when I see your answering heart I know
you mean the same.

We grew out of braces and bikes
and Famous Five escapades.
Ships in the night, we pass each other
In the pitch black dark—
I send up a firework
for you and you alone.

An Adventure

Follow the black cat. It purrs
and clings to your calves
Follow it, as it pads

Through the exit of your
concrete building,
through the wooden door
sheathed in ivy

Stroke its tail once,
twice to send it away;
Feel the moss-carpet grow through your toes
the vines curl into your skin.

Let balmy osmanthus air
make house inside your nose
Rivers of molten stars
Replace your blood.

Let clothes fall apart
Petals against your skin,
instead.
Let the widows and brides
Red and yellow and purple hoods

Lay leaf-blankets over you
Weave their hats into your hair.
Let the honey-milk they give

Soothe your soul.

Fall into slumber,
So deep and bejewelled
Dimmed stars lining
Backs of your lids.

Let your body fall through
soil, mud
pool with quiet rain
Melt and mingle with the grass
Until you and it are one and the same.

Sweatshirt

My sweatshirt reeks
of your acrid touch.
Laundered, sprayed, showered
It lingers like oil on wood.

The memory slices like a knife
old, faded, rusted sharp
cuts through my skin
precise as a surgeon.

I bathed four times
that day. Locked myself
in my room in the crevices
of my mind, and burned every thought.

Yesterday I found it in the back of a cupboard
Never changed, exactly the same.
It was such a comfortable sweatshirt.
A real shame
I never wore it again.

Soles and Souls

On the six pm train from east to west
Last tuesday I saw seven shoes.

The first, bright white, three stripes
and laces, mirroring two
pairs of the same.

Low burgundy heels, creased
At the toes, lifted
for arms to encircle a neck.

White plastic bags rest, briefly
on a slippered foot
blue-green striped rubber;
tired after a long day.

Rough black boots
Caked in dust and grime
Heels to dig into cement and slime.

Boots of a different kind
Shiny and new, the yellow stitching
speaking volumes if you
cared to look.

Neon pink cleats,
sole upside-down mountained
valleys of mud in
crevices — rank with sweat.

My own, black and white
crocs : a practical choice
The same I used to wade in
pools of rainwater when i was a child.

Coffee in ten

"Order?"   "Yeah! I'll have a mocha with whipped cream, please."
"To go?"   "Having here! I'm spending time with my boyfriend."
"Sir, Your order?   "The same." I could never resist her.
"Uh, Mocha. To go."   Across the table, she blew kisses.
This time I was alone.   I held her hand, gently.
Couldn't stop going to our shop.   Two more weeks, until
the mocha tasted bitter. Drank it anyway.   She broke me.
Our thing, left to me like a mockery.   I stayed
Me, A Mocha and the sick, jeering February breeze.   Suffocating.

When in Fairprice

“Turmeric, Beans.”
“What?” a confused, slightly wary look.
“I need—,”A ball of bile, spiders on skin
sweat beaded forehead.

“I—I, uh. I don’t know..”
So foggy. Why were there…aisles?
She’d definitely
been here before—

A memory curled
at the edges of consciousness
wispy, fleeting
fleeing on sight.

Right. Grocery shopping.
Darling Nate’s
homecoming.
She would make beans
his favourite.

Water-heavy legs
ached and moaned.
A blink. Head crowded —
thunder! A flash!

She was at checkout.
How….?

When had she bought
A hot wheels set?

"Everything all right, Mrs. D'Souza?"
"Oh! Yes...I'm buying beans for my son."
"Oh yes, his Saturday meal! Your cooking is
delicious, he'll love it."

In her living room her Nathaniel waited
still on the wall, framed
and garlanded.

Four Pillars

The first left cuff —
solid, heavy, rusty iron.
the hand that locked it :
wrinkled and grey.

robed in silver, gold ornate
red vermillion to mark my end.
as he left the room was drenched
with sickly sweet incense.

My right hand leadened
Another click, a key.
this time a familiar face.
like water, the eyes, the nose, the ears
different, yet
a mirror unto my own.

The third one moved in creaks and grunts
ancient bones, no longer lithe.
in his walk his feet left marks
even on the stone floor.

Two ankles this time, he bent
on his back stood a thousand men
hate and anger seething they
cried loudly, "Conform!"

the spikes dug into my flesh

spilling jewelled blood
thick and slow it still
caught the scanty prison light.

The last to enter shocked me still.
In the gait I saw my feet.
In her mouth I saw my teeth.
her hands, fingers, five of mine
I knew it then — it was I.

My apparition drew
closer to my neck.
With her hands and sorrowful face
She squeezed my throat until I gave.

Long after, at my dying breath
from a corner of my eye I spied
a glistening tear on her cheek.

On Jealousy

Sometimes I wonder
If the screen I stare into
is brighter than my future.

I write; I pour
my whole soul into every word
another grasps its essence

and shapes it better than I ever could.

something claws in my ribcage, then
vile, filthy, bitter acid
it gnaws on
my bones for years and years
every time I put words to page.

In the scale of the incomprehensible cosmos I am
little
I understand, Must
I be so little in my
own domain?

I am God
If God created the Earth
and humans surpassed him.

Shake me by the shoulders
Fall to my feet
And tell me I am enough,
I beg.

Cafeteria Confessional

A hundred people chatter but only your voice is worth hearing. my heart thunders in my ears, my throat clogs. do you feel it, too? the burning in the air, your skin, your cheeks. something like fear forms in my blood. your gaze is anything but predatory. grey floor beneath us morphing into roiling waves, the christmas decorations dissipating foam, we, a pair of buoys, solitary on a stormy night. do you see it too? do you look at me, too, and see the same stardust of which you were made? there is something ancient in you i recognise. do you look at me and ache to reach over and hold me like the rays of a dying sun grasp desperately at a bloody horizon? like a victim stabbed clutches the knife holding in his guts?

will you be a welcome wound, or will you leave me bleeding?

Kintsugi

I used to do pottery.
bowls, mugs, plates
with every gentle push and pull
I stepped into sacred skin
.

I gave them names. Ruchi
after my mother, Raksha, Nandini
I remember the Thursday
evening I broke Dahlia.

Rage made me strong, I threw
her across the room with ease.
I watched : petaled rim touched
a wall. Fell and
cracked to five.

For one horrible moment I felt no regret
then I sank to the floor and cried.
quietly, then I fetched a broom
and swept the shards together.

My wheel grew dry and dusty.
My studio dull and void.
I touched not one plate I had made
Lest it crumble to ash.

Every night I wept and seethed
sequestered solitary selfish leech
guilt, dejection clawed me hollow
day by day and week by week.

Greater monsters have created art
Greater angels it destroyed.
When my hands stopped trembling
They ached to create.

brush and gold and plaster
shard by shard and stroke by stroke
I painted dahlias in gold
and repaired a broken plate.

Comets

I look up at the night sky at
the blazing trail of green light and wonder sometimes
if the girl who watched it fifty thousand years ago
stood there
in the pitch black night and wondered if a girl
her age, fifty thousand years later would stare at

the same, yet different sky
the same, yet different comet.

this is the last time humanity will ever see it, the
last time I will be able to see something my ancestors
saw.
then i remember, i am wrong
i am wrong! and so happy for it. every day i see
the earth my ancestors touched. the mountains they
climbed
the moon they wrote poetry about. the trees they
planted the
fire they passed on to me in the matchbox on my
nightstand.
every time i breathe the air i remember the songs they
sang once lived in it.
when i sink my toes into warm wet mud i remember i
am standing on their graves
and their bodies still nourish life. if they were here i
would

show them my school and brick and mortar house
and
instant coffee and hot chocolate and
my water bottle which keeps my cold water cold and
my
hot water hot and the array of spices from all over the
world I keep in my kitchen

and say, “we have thrived,”

and i wonder if fifty thousand years later
a girl my age will think the same.

I am Still in Here

stop. peel the layers from what you see
one by one, slowly. try, for my sake
and you will see
i am still in here.

for all you have done to me i deserve it.
i persist, despite, and persistence
must not be hidden.

walk not with closed eyes, but open them
and see that i am
still in here.

look past skin and muscle and blood
and see my spirit within, my drive
my willpower, my joy,
my laughter
and know that I am Still in here.

like the moon i wax and wane
the light inside me never dims.
i live, i laugh, i hurt, i cry
i long to be seen.

reach your soul out to mine
shed all preconceptions
all prejudice, all fear
see me for who i am and realise
i am still in here.

Dealing with Humans

1. The sea under blinding sunlight — freeze it.
2. thread the edges with blue and red ribbon. pay attention to every interwoven thread. watch as it emerges and descends, over and over again like a dolphin in an ocean. like a dancer in the throes of emotion, like the brush-strokes of an artist drawing a soul.
3. this is crucial. weigh it. these directions will be of no use if doing this bankrupts you.
4. if the weight is fairly light — it won't cost a lot —- proceed with this step. go south to the beach you grew up near, and ask the water for some of its foam. If it is kind enough to oblige, carry it back, carefully, and press it under a trigonometry textbook.
5. After four hours, it should come out looking like a triangle. Affix this to the rectangle of sea you froze in step 1. you will notice it is flexible and iridescent. if the sea has been generous it will sing you a song every time you bend it.
6. next, take a sheet of paper. Any kind will do. You are sending this to a human, after all. Hold it out to the flowers and ask them to breathe on it. Once, Twice, Thrice should be enough.
7. A side effect of this, if you are lucky, is that the flowers will sneeze and shed petals.

Gather them quickly, before they sink into the soil, and add them to the hollow of your frozen sea.

8. This ingredient might be hard to find — human ink. If you cannot find it, squid ink will suffice.
9. Now it is all subjective. Feel the paper. Think about the human you wish to approach. Pay attention to your breath, your heart. Do you feel light? Effervescent? Does the air feel warm or chilly? Do the flowers seem brighter, larger somehow? In your heart of hearts (no, not that one. The one next to it. Yes.) find the words you wish to write. Catch them lazily, slowly like a butterfly-catcher catches butterflies. Pounce on them when you can, lest they disappear in a fit of cowardice.
10. Once you have written on the paper and folded it into your animal of choice, introduce it to your frozen sea. An interesting fact about the frozen sea : it is called an envy-lope. It has no connection to antelopes. Once you have carefully situated your animal with flowers (optional) and plenty of food for the journey, bid it farewell. Remember to treat it kindly, for it will tell the human if you don't.
11. Fold over the sea foam, closing the opening of the hollow. Gather pollen from the flowers : I personally like lavender and tulips for this. Melt it over an open fire until

it forms a soft coin. Use this coin to buy wax from the crow living in your attic (a surprise? I thought you knew! He's been there for a year now!) and seal the envelope with wax and lavender.

12. Go out. Call thrice for a mouse in your language. A mongoose will arrive. Do not be confused, and do not correct the mongoose when it answers to mouse. Hand it your letter, and whisper in its ear the description of the human's house.
13. Be sure to hand it some cheese to keep up the ruse, and watch it until it disappears from your eyesight. If it knows you are watching, it will not wander.
14. And now we wait.

praise and person

neck lace
perfect spheres
perfect eyes
orange smooth
supermarket lights
tape and measure
stretch and measure
taped measure
file trim polish
wax shave dust
bleach brighten
raw ripen
perfect phasic paradox
smoothen straighten
iron steam perfect
curve perfect seam
pearl white pearl bright
pearl smooth pearl silky
perfect light perfect mic
heart shrivel
smile bright
seven seconds
whole life.

No One Likes Runtime Errors

```
import java.faith;
import java.embryo;
public class organ{
public static void uterus(String args[]){
Scanner sc=new Scanner(System.in);
int baby = 360;
int i=0;
boolean breathe, scream = false;
boolean grief=false;
int fate;
while(i<baby)
{
breathe=true;
scream=true;
System.out.println(“Push!”);
i++;
System.out.println(“Will you take it? Enter 1 for yes,
0 for no”);
fate=sc.nextInt();
faith.God();
if(fate==0) {System.exit(0);grief=true;}
}
print(“Survival!”);
print(“You gave birth!”);
System.exit(0);
}
}
```

Claustrophobia

knockknockknock
heaving. hoarse throat
i might have to
drink my sweat
at this point.

knockknockknockknock!
are you deaf? why are you just
sitting there reading right
by that lampshade? can you not
hear me? hear
ME?

maybe i should
use a chair
BOOM! KNOCKKNOCK
NO! a look around is
all i get?

"The neighbours are being
noisy
again!"

nononotthem!!! im INSIDE
INSIDETHEWALLSYOUHUNGYOURPAINTING
SON
peel the wallpaper axe the plaster
free me from this

cl a u s t r
o p h o b i
a
let
me

out
!

knock. knock.
knock knock knock
knock kn

I DONT HAVE AIR ICANTBREATHEIMTRYING
ONE TWO THREE
FOUR.. FIVE....
i dont know if i can
go on much longer...
let
me
out

Ask me not to Stand my Ground

Ask me not to stand my ground.
my heels are cracked, my
stance is faltering

Ask me not to stand my ground
we both know
there will be no end.

Ask me not to stand my ground
my blood has run, my corpse is husk
the mud has imprints of my heels.

Ask me not to stand my ground
repel me with all your might
winds and waves and storms

I will face them all.

Ask me not to stand my ground
it is what you do not want
That I know so
I will not relent.

Ask me not to stand my ground
I will not budge until I am gone
and in my place, my
ghost will follow.

www.ingramcontent.com/pod-product-compliance
Lightning Source LLC
Chambersburg PA
CBHW051744130826
49812CB00033B/997